Planet Earth

Oceans

Steve Parker

QED Publishing

Copyright © QED Publishing 2008

First published in the UK in 2008 by
QED Publishing
A Quarto Group company
226 City Road
London EC1V 2TT

www.qed-publishing.co.uk

A catalogue record for this book is
available from the British Library.

ISBN 978 1 84538 956 7

Author Steve Parker
Design and Editorial East River Partnership

Publisher Steve Evans
Creative Director Zeta Davies

Printed and bound in China

Words in **bold** are
explained in the
glossary on page 30.

Contents

Wet world

Only 30 percent of the Earth's surface is made up of earth and rocks. The other 70 percent consists of water in rivers, lakes, seas and oceans.

Salty water

Most of the world's water is the salty water of the seas and oceans. This includes warm, shallow **bays** and colourful, **tropical reefs** as well as the huge, wide-open expanses and cold, dark depths of the oceans.

It's so... big!

The world's largest ocean is the Pacific. It covers one-third of the world – 18 times larger than the USA and more than 700 times larger than the UK!

Tropical islands are surrounded by a vast ocean.

Wow!

The five oceans are:
Pacific (180 million km²)
Atlantic (106 million km²)
Indian (73 million km²)
Southern (20 million km²)
Arctic (14 million km²)

On a rescue mission, the coast guard often has to battle stormy seas.

Mysterious oceans

Oceans are the largest areas of salty water. Seas, such as the Caribbean and Mediterranean, are smaller and are partly surrounded by land. The oceans are so vast that there is still plenty of exploring to do. Many mysteries lurk in their depths!

Marlin are among the largest, fastest fish in the world's oceans.

Arctic Ocean

Atlantic Ocean

Mediterranean Sea

Caribbean Sea

Equator

Pacific Ocean

Indian Ocean

Southern Ocean

5

Tide ins and outs

The water level in oceans and seas does not stay the same. It goes up and down twice a day. This movement is known as the tide.

At high tide, waves lap against the quayside.

Effect of gravity

Tides are caused by the movement of the Earth and Moon and by a pulling force called **gravity**. The Earth's gravity keeps everything on its surface. The Moon's gravity pulls the Earth's ocean water towards it, which forms a slight bulge of water in the Earth's oceans.

Water levels

High tides are caused by the bulge of water in the oceans. As the Earth continues to turn, the water level goes down again. This is called **low tide**. Tides can move plants and animals along the shore, as well as ships in harbours and ports.

At low tide, small boats sit out of the water.

Wow!

Canada's Bay of Fundy has the biggest tides. The difference between high and low tide is 16 metres, the same as ten people standing on each other's heads!

Very low tides can leave ships stuck near the shore.

It's so... confusing!

Spring tides are extra-high tides that occur every two weeks, when the Sun lines up with the Moon. They do not just happen in spring!

Meet the sea

Without rivers, seas and oceans around the world would dry up. Luckily, rivers pour water into them and keep them topped up.

Pelicans feed on the fish that swim in estuary waters.

Sand and mud

As rivers get close to the sea, they widen into a mouth called an **estuary**, or bay. Rivers carry tiny pieces of sand and mud. Near the sea, rivers slow down and the sand and mud fall to the bottom. This is why estuaries and bays often have shallow mud flats, salt marshes and sandbanks.

A saltwater crocodile warms up on a mudbank before sliding into the water.

Wow!

About one-fifth of all the river water that flows into the world's oceans every day comes from the huge Amazon River.

In summer, flowers bloom on salt marshes.

Teeming with life

Although the surface of the mud and sand may look bare, underneath it is teeming with life. Here, creatures, such as worms, shrimps, crabs and shellfish, live in huge numbers. As the tide comes in, these animals come out to feed on tiny bits of food. But when they do this, they are in danger from hungry fish and birds.

Fiddler crabs live in salty marshes.

It's so big!

The world's biggest reptile is the estuarine crocodile, also called the saltwater crocodile. It lives around South-east Asia and Australia, and grows to be 7 metres long.

On the beach

Sea currents, waves and tides not only move sand and pebbles on a beach, they also wash up seaweed, animals and litter.

Weeverfish bury themselves in sand.

Sea lions crowd onto beaches to rest.

Strong currents

Sand is made up of tiny bits of broken rock and animal shells. Waves and water movements, called **currents**, move this sand around. Although small waves and light currents leave the sand in place, larger waves and strong currents can wash sand away to leave larger bits called shingle.

Wading birds search for food in sand and mud.

Bits and pieces

As the tide rises and then falls, it washes up many things, including straggly seaweed, dead fish, starfish, shells and driftwood. This area is called the **strandline**. Unfortunately, you will usually also find man-made rubbish, such as plastic bottles and bags.

Wow!

Sea turtles, which are now very rare, lay eggs in beach sand. Their babies hatch out a few weeks later and run to the sea.

Baby turtles race to the sea before gulls, crabs, lizards and other animals eat them.

Cliffs and rocky shores

Where ocean waves crash against hard rocks, they form tall cliffs and rock pools below. These are home for large numbers of animals.

Waves can wear rocks into amazing shapes, such as these tall sea stacks.

Cliff-nesting birds are safe from many enemies.

Tall cliffs

Although cliffs and rocky shores can be dangerous places, many creatures live here. Birds, such as gannets, razorbills and guillemots, nest on tiny ledges along steep cliffs. They fly out to sea to catch fish for their chicks.

Anemones look like flowers, but most are poisonous.

Rock pools

As the tide goes out, it leaves small pools among the rocks. These teem with all kinds of animals. Crabs hide under stones, and blennies, gobies and other fish take cover among slippery seaweed. Anemones sting shrimps and tiny fish with their tentacles.

Wow!

In Australia, the blue-ringed octopus lives in rock pools. It is very small, but has a deadly bite. It has enough poison to kill ten people!

It's so... tall!

The tallest sea cliffs are at Kalaupapa in Hawaii. They tower 1000 metres above the sea. This is 2.5 times higher than New York's Empire State Building and three times higher than France's Eiffel Tower.

In the shallows

Around many coasts are areas of sea less than 200 metres deep. Here, rather than the deep ocean, is where most sea creatures live.

Manatees live in shallow and warm bays, estuaries and lagoons.

Sunlight and nutrients

Plants, such as eel grass, wracks and oarweeds, grow well in shallow waters. This is because lots of sunlight reaches the bottom and plenty of **nutrients** are deposited by rivers. These plants provide food and shelter for all kinds of small animals, such as fish, crabs, worms and shellfish.

Seaweeds, such as bladderwrack and hollow green-weed, form beautiful underwater gardens.

14

Wow!

The manatee, also called the sea cow, eats sea grass. The manatee has flippers and a round tail, and grows to be as large as a real cow!

Plaice can change colour to look like sand.

Hunting in the shallows

Larger creatures, such as octopuses, seals and porpoises, hunt among the weeds and rocks. Flatfish, such as plaice, soles and flounders, also search for **prey**. These fish lie hidden on the seafloor and wait for their prey to come near. Then they pounce.

The octopus grabs prey with eight suckered tentacles.

It's so... long!

Jellyfish are simple creatures with no skeleton, brain or heart. Some have very long stinging tentacles with which they catch fish and other prey.

Colourful corals

Coral reefs grow where the water is warm, shallow and clear. Reefs have more kinds of wildlife than any other place in the sea.

Stony cups

Coral reefs are huge rocks with lots of cracks, caves and ledges. Tiny coral animals build stony cups around themselves for protection and when they die, they leave behind the hard cups. These build up into the reef. Different kinds of corals make different shapes, including mushrooms, vases, tubes, horns and fans.

Few places are as colourful as a coral reef.

Coral creatures have stinging tentacles.

It's so... threatened!

Coral reefs face many dangers, including people collecting their corals and shells and damage caused by boats. Mud and silt deposits also kill the tiny coral animals.

Prowling the reef

Fish and shrimps swim among the coral, along with starfish, sea urchins and worms. Their bright colours make them easy to see by others of their kind. Sharks, such as the black-tipped reef shark, prowl around the reef edge, waiting to snap up prey.

Giant groupers can swallow other fish whole.

Wow!

One of the biggest reef fish is the giant grouper, which has a mouth as big as wheelie bin!

Sea horses are fish that swim slowly and suck in tiny bits of food.

Moving and breathing

Animals need to breathe oxygen to stay alive. Some sea creatures breathe air like humans, while others breathe underwater using gills.

Taking a breath

Sea animals that breathe air include whales, dolphins, seals, sea lions, turtles and sea snakes. They come to the surface now and then to take a breath. If they are unlucky enough to get trapped under the water's surface by fishing nets, they drown.

Dolphins breathe through the blowhole on top of their head.

Wow!

Some whales can hold their breath for more than two hours when they dive deep into the ocean to search for food!

Sea snakes swim by wriggling through the water.

Using gills

Fish, squid, sea worms and starfish all breathe underwater. They have frilly tissues called gills, which take in **oxygen** from the water. On most fish, the gills are found under slits on each side of the front part of their body.

Speedy squid can swim through the water quickly.

Moving around

Animals in the sea move in different ways. Fish swish their fins and tail, whales flap their flukes, or tail, and crabs run sideways. A squid pushes itself through the water by squirting water.

It's so... fast!

The oceans' fastest swimmer is the sailfish. It can swim at more than 100 kilometres an hour, almost as fast as the cheetah can run.

The open ocean

The oceans contain billions of tiny creatures, such as the copepod.

In the open ocean, there is nowhere to hide. Animals that live here have to cope with big waves, hot sun and predators of all kinds.

Phytoplankton are plants. They are too small to be seen without a microscope.

Whale sharks swim slowly through the water as they feed.

It's so... massive!

The largest fish is the whale shark. At 12 metres long, it is as big as a school bus. But it is not dangerous. It feeds on tiny creatures called plankton.

Killer whales hunt many creatures, including seals, fish and seabirds.

Plant plankton

There are few seaweeds in the open ocean, but there are billions of minuscule plants called **phytoplankton**. These are eaten by very small animals, who are then food for small fish, squid and other creatures. Larger fish eat these, and are in turn food for bigger creatures, right up to the largest ocean hunters such as the great white shark and killer whale.

Wow!

The world's largest hunter is the sperm whale. It grows up to 18 metres long and can weigh up to 50,000 kilograms – the same as seven African elephants!

Twilight zone

Far below the ocean surface is a dim and gloomy world. Here, animals have big eyes to see in the half-light of the dark depths.

Strange creatures

Deeper in the ocean there is less sunlight, so plants cannot grow. Some amazing creatures live here, including strange fish, jellyfish, worms, squid and octopuses. These animals swim or drift all their lives and never touch anything solid. They eat dead creatures that drift down from above, or hunt and eat each other.

It's so weird!

The nautilus, a cousin of the octopus, has a stripy coiled shell. It has big eyes to see in the gloom and more than 80 tentacles to catch fish.

Flashlight fish have an area, just below each eye, that glows.

Wow!

Weddell seals can dive to a depth of 600 metres. Their excellent eyesight enables them to see in these dimly lit depths.

Many jellyfish produce a bright, luminous light.

Making light

Not all deep-water animals need light. Some sea animals glow in the dark! They have special body parts that make light. This is called **bioluminescence**. Flashlight fish have shining eyes, and lanternfish have spots of light along the body. There are also glowing jellyfish and squid.

Bottom of the sea

In the deepest parts of the ocean, there is no day or night, and no winter or summer. It is dark and cold all the time.

Dark region

The sun's light and warmth cannot reach deeper than 500 metres beneath the surface of the ocean. Below this, it is cold and black. This vast region is the largest place in the world. Many creatures, such as fish, squid, jellyfish and shellfish, live here.

It's so... hot!

In some places on the seabed, boiling water spurts through vents. Here, there are giant worms as thick as your arm and as long as a car.

Wow!!

The ocean's deepest place is the Mariana Trench in the north-west Pacific. It goes down 10,923 metres. Mount Everest would fit here with over 2000 metres to spare!

Underwater craft, called submersibles, explore the seabed.

The anglerfish uses a glowing light to attract fish.

Ghostly fish

On the bottom of the deep sea there are rocky mountains, cliffs, flat plains of mud, valleys and **canyons**. Here live deep-sea starfish, sea cucumbers, white crabs and pale, ghostly fish. Many animals are blind as there is no light, making eyes of no use.

Crabs, worms and shellfish gather around hot water rising from a deep-sea vent.

25

Using the oceans

Seas and oceans are very useful for people, and not just for water sports and seaside holidays.

Fishing

The world's oceans are busy with fishing boats that catch huge amounts of fish and shellfish. Seafood is especially important for people who live on small islands as it provides them with food and something to sell.

Many Asian fishermen use traps to catch fish.

A wind turbine's blades rotate to turn wind power into electricity.

Wind power

The wind out at sea is very useful to us. It whips across the oceans much faster than it does over land. A huge machine, called a turbine, turns the power of the wind into another kind of power – electricity.

The world's biggest ship has a deck so huge, it could hold four football pitches.

Tsunamis cause terrible damage and loss of life.

Container ships carry goods in big, steel boxes.

Shipping

Oceans provide routes for the enormous ships that carry cargo from port to port. Containers on these ships are filled with all kinds of goods, from cars and shoes to toys and frozen food. Air transport is faster, but it is much cheaper to send goods by ship, and ships can carry greater weights, too.

Seas and oceans at risk

Oceans and seas are in trouble. We throw rubbish into them, pollute them with chemicals and catch too much of their wildlife.

Damaged by pollution

Seas and oceans are becoming more and more polluted. People litter the beach and dump rubbish overboard from ships and boats. Pipes from factories pour in dangerous chemicals. A giant oil tanker may have an accident and spill its thick, black oil. This floats on the sea and kills fish, seabirds and other wildlife.

Flooding lowlands

The problem of **global warming** will greatly affect seas and oceans all around the world. This warming may cause water to expand and the ice at the poles to melt. This could raise ocean levels and flood low-lying areas of land, making millions of people homeless.

Birds affected by oil spills cannot fly or catch food.

In the future, coastal flooding may well happen more often.

It's so... dangerous!

Plastic bags floating in the sea look similar to jellyfish. Sea turtles eat jellyfish, but if they swallow a plastic bag by mistake, they may die.

Litter left or washed up on a beach can harm wildlife.

29

Glossary

Bay Part of a coast that curves around an area of sea.

Bioluminescence When living things produce light by special chemical processes.

Canyon Very deep, steep-sided valley.

Current Flowing movements in water.

Estuary The end, or mouth, of a river, where it widens and flows into the sea.

Global warming Heating up of the Earth caused by changes in the gases that make up its atmosphere.

Gravity The pulling force coming from all things, especially large objects such as the Earth and Moon.

High tide The highest level reached by the sea. High tide happens twice a day.

Low tide The lowest level of the sea. Low tide is reached twice a day.

Nutrients Substances used as food by living things.

Oxygen A gas that is in the air we breathe. Oxygen is also found in water and is used by underwater creatures to breathe.

Phytoplankton Tiny plants, mostly too small to see, that float in seas, oceans and large lakes.

Prey An animal that is hunted for food.

Reef A large, rocky part of the seabed, usually built by tiny coral animals.

Strandline The long, thin heap of washed-up things along the shore, which is left by high tides.

Tropical Around the middle of the world, in the region called the tropics, where it is very warm all year.

Tsunami A series of huge waves that is set off by underwater earthquakes.

Vapour In the form of a gas that floats and changes shape.

Index